THE THREE DIMENSIONS OF A MAGNIFICENT BLACK WOMAN

THE
THREE DIMENSIONS
OF A
MAGNIFICENT
BLACK
WOMAN

AN INSPIRATION TO SUCCEED

A. MARIE NEALY

authorHOUSE®

AuthorHouse™
1663 Liberty Drive
Bloomington, IN 47403
www.authorhouse.com
Phone: 1-800-839-8640

Published by AuthorHouse 6/24/2013

ISBN: 978-1-4817-6675-3 (sc)
ISBN: 978-1-4817-6664-7 (e)

Library of Congress Control Number: 2013911081

This book is dedicated to you.

Preface

Who am I, and why should you listen to me? I am a black woman, and I am well aware of the obstacles we face. A lot of my knowledge came from education, but much of it comes from experience. I have struggled through trials, frustration, and rejection. But I made it. I wrote this book to inspire our women to achieve greatness in spite of what they face. This book is the product of observing black women in the congregation and education system where I have been a pastor and have taught for many years. I noticed that many of the young ladies and older women lacked the self-confidence and positive thinking to make things happen in their lives. Many times, I saw that goals were not being pursued, and it seemed that there was no desire to excel. It seemed as though their spirits had been broken. Believe me, I have sat listening to many of our women say, "I have not accomplished anything in my life; I have not been productive at all." I hope that will not be said again. To look back on a life well spent is one of God's greatest gifts.

It is my desire here to show appreciation for my mother. It is because of her love, inspiration, and wisdom that I am so grateful. It is her devotion to God that continues to push me forward in the work that I have embarked upon. I want to thank my daughters, Andrea Grant and Robyn Scates, as well as my son-in-law, Terry Scates, who are always there to encourage me in all endeavors. I am grateful to Lauren Thomas, my editor, who does not fail to give me constructive criticism. I also want to thank my dear friend, McKinley Newsom, for taking the time to read my manuscripts. Last but not least, I want to thank my friend, Charles Branch, for his patience and commitment to my work and vision. I feel a deep sense of gratitude toward Dr. Susie Tucker (deceased), for relentlessly being in my corner, and my cousin, Robert Simmons, for pushing me to finish this book.

Contents

Introduction

This book was written for black women who seek guidance in developing the confidence needed to succeed in a world that presents a vast array of experiences, which includes obstacles that often impact how they view or rate themselves. Unfortunately, some black women do not feel beautiful unless they are conforming to white aesthetic standards. I hope that reading this book will help you see yourself as beautiful so you can develop the positive thinking and confidence that God wants you to have as you cope and survive in a society that can make black women feel unacceptable. I want you to understand that God wants you to be equipped with self-confidence, and he wants you to have a sense of self-beauty.

Facing difficult situations with fear is a learned behavior, but you must realize that this fear factor can hold you back. You learn to face the fear of tackling difficult situations by asserting effort, believing that you are capable, seeing yourself as beautiful, refusing to accept that your goals are impossible, acquiring the skills you need to accomplish your goals, and having a strong faith in God, who wants you to succeed in your endeavors. When you embrace faith in God, you become strengthened to move aside the barrier to success that comes from fear. With a spirit of endurance, you can change your life and foster a positive outcome in the lives of others you encounter.

This book contains Christian teachings that aim to help you develop positive thinking. As you begin to think in a positive manner, your self-confidence will increase. A black woman must see herself as beautiful, both physically and spiritually. It is said that beauty is in the eye of the beholder. So why not see yourself as beautiful? When you do, your spirit glows.

I encourage you to "trust in the Lord with all thine heart; and lean not unto thine own understanding. In all thy ways acknowledge him, and he shall direct thy paths" (Proverbs 3:5–6, KJV). Look to God through prayer for everything you do. Trust him. God will guide. To acknowledge God is to realize that his hand is at work in every part of your life. Therefore, when you are successful, give him the glory.

The Three Dimensions of a Magnificent Black Woman addresses the concerns of black women that I have observed and spoken with over many years in the congregation, at work, in schools, and in the community. I conducted a survey of two hundred black women who expressed an interest in learning ways to improve themselves. They revealed that spirituality is an important factor in their lives. They were concerned that media images of beautiful women often overlook and exclude black women. Media displays the beautiful woman as having lighter skin, thin lips, straight hair and a thin body. The perception of beautiful women created by media can generate a sense of self-doubt and fear of not being accepted, regardless of economic status and education level. A woman's economic status or education level doesn't predict self-doubt or a fear of being accepted, nor does it ensure that she will possess self-confidence and will be fearless. In this book, I have addressed how to overcome these feelings. The impact of exclusion and the stereotypical labels, such as "the angry black woman" or "the strong black woman," are designed to trigger self- doubt. Are you angry because you are a black woman whose nature is to be angry, or are you simply experiencing a human emotion that has caused you anger at a particular time? Are you strong because you are a black woman and white women are not strong, or are you exhibiting strength because fear won't help you meet your goal? These stereotypes will only hinder you if you allow them to. When your spirit is strong and you have faith in the Lord, you can combat negativity with self-assuredness. Jesus wants black women to be women with self-confidence who accomplish greatness with the Lord's love and guidance.

I hope that this book will be helpful and inspire you to reach your desired greatness. I want you to learn to love, support, and encourage other black women as you work toward your goals. I pray for you to learn to lean on God for success. He is the Creator. He loves all and knows everyone's destiny. After reading this book, I hope it will become a companion piece to remind you to live as a positive, self-confident, and beautiful black woman. We who seek to offer black women some constructive inspiration that will bolster their feeling of self-worth will find *The Three Dimensions of a Magnificent Black Woman* useful when conducting seminars, ministering, or conducting other types of counsel. When our three dimensions of positive thinking, self-confidence, and beauty of body and spirit are realized, we all are magnificent black women!

Chapter 1

The Positive-Thinking Woman

Our minds hold the power that shapes what we do in life. Whether our thoughts are positive or negative, we are shaped by what we think. James Allen says in his book *As You Think*, "We are literally what we think, our character being the complete sum of all our thoughts."[1] What it all boils down to is one's thoughts form what one is or what one becomes. Who is the positive-thinking woman? Is that you or someone you would like to be? Do you find yourself thinking negatively and uttering negative comments? Do you know that there is a divine presence in your life that is always present? Was positive thinking nurtured in you from the beginning? Were you made to feel good about yourself?

When you come into this life, your mind is like a blank sheet of paper. It is truly up to parents and other meaningful individuals to write something on that blank sheet and to provide positive reinforcement. It is up to them to prepare the child for the challenges of life and to foster positive thinking. When this is not done, life experiences can sometimes bring about counterproductive results. Now, of course, children don't always heed the lessons parents teach them, but at least if they are presented, the chances of those lessons kicking in at opportune times are heightened. All children need nurturing by those significant people

---

1 James Allen, As You Think: Second Edition, (Novato, CA, New World Library, the edited Version by Marc Allen, 1998) 23.

that surround them on a daily basis. The importance of self-esteem should be instilled. A child should be encouraged to reach for the stars and engaged in discussions about the talents that God has bestowed upon each person.

Hopefully, the adults that surround the child do not squash her dreams. It is important that a positive-thinking child matures and embraces this characteristic as an adult. In spite of these parental initiatives, some may acquire feelings of self-doubt that damage their self-confidence and ability to succeed in the world. Of course, some have not had parental or significant people encouragement. However, it is never too late to undergo transformation.

This book is written for black women, young and old, who are seriously seeking to think positively. If you are a young woman who wants to develop into a positive, strong, beautiful, and confident black woman, this book provides some practical steps that will help you reach your goals. I hope that the more mature black women who never acquired these attributes or who have begun to doubt their magnificence will find this book a helpful refresher. I also hope that it will be an inspiration to dispel any doubts you may have about yourself. It will help if you know that there is a God who promises to be with you through it all. You can transform your life. I want you to be able to develop into that positive, confident, beautiful, and successful woman that God intended you to be.

In this day and time, many of us face so many problems, challenges, and fears along with competition and jealousy. Whether you know it or not, we continue to live in a country where racial discrimination continues to exist. There are many doubts about the future. There are worries about the financial status of the country as well as the enormous amount of societal ills in the community and the world. However, we have to remember that we are profoundly blessed, and we can keep a positive outlook on life. I am not suggesting that you deny the truth because you must acknowledge what is actually happening around you. Things are definitely going to go wrong. There will be certain forces in life that you cannot control, such as social, political, and economic conditions. However, there are conditions that you can adjust to in life.

Life is full of trials and tribulations, and you definitely have to deal with them. Do not allow trouble to immobilize you and stop progress. When you are a positive thinker, you can recreate what you want in life. If you are not satisfied with your position in life and don't have a sense of accomplishment, then you must change the direction you have taken. This is positive thinking. No matter what happens, things will turn out alright. As a black woman, you have the ability to accomplish whatever it is you want to achieve. The mind is the key component to believing that what seems impossible is indeed possible. You must expect that things will turn out alright. You will focus on the goal. A good example of this is found in the story of the Apostle Paul, who found immense strength and courage in God.

He preached,

"I am more; in labours more abundant, in stripes above measure, in prisons more frequent, in deaths oft. Of the Jews five times received I forty stripes save one. Thrice was I beaten with rods, once was I stoned, thrice I suffered shipwreck, a night and a day I have been in the deep, in journeyings often, in perils of waters, in perils of robbers, in perils by mine own countrymen, in perils by the heathen, in perils in the city, in perils in the wilderness, in perils in the sea, in perils among false brethren; In weariness and painfulness, in watchings often, in hunger and thirst, in fastings often, in cold and nakedness. Beside those things that are without, that which cometh upon me daily, the care of all the churches. Who is weak, and I am not weak? Who is offended, and I burn not? If I must needs glory, I will glory of the things which concern mine infirmities. I must boast about myself, except about my weaknesses....[God] said to me, 'My grace is sufficient for thee: for my strength is made perfect in weakness.' Most gladly therefore will I rather glory in my infirmities, that the power of Christ may rest on me. Therefore I take pleasure in infirmities, in reproaches, in necessities, in persecutions, in distresses for Christ's sake: for when I am weak, then I am strong" (2 Corinthians 11:23–12:10, KJV).

Through all of the troubles Paul experienced, he let nothing stop him from his goal at hand, which was his ministry. Paul was a positive thinker, and he believed that he could achieve the goal that Christ called him to conquer. His task was not easy, but Paul truly believed he could endure. Christ called him to preach the Gospel, and he did.

Paul encountered rejections and humiliating situations that would make some people forget about what they were trying to achieve. Like Paul, many human beings have suffered adversities in life, but know God does not want you to be weak, passive, or ineffective. In spite of hardships, like Paul, you can endure and will accomplish what you set out to do when you have faith. And remember: your strength comes from God.

Let us take a look at the journey of some black women who have soared to great heights. Toni Morrison overcame divorce and other obstacles to become a renowned writer who holds a Pulitzer Prize and the Nobel Prize for Literature. Oprah Winfrey rose from poverty and trouble in her formative years to become one of the most powerful women in television, and she is very wealthy. Maya Angelou soared to great heights after a troubled time in her youth when she was raped by her mother's boyfriend. As a renowned writer, actress, and professor, Maya is truly an example of what one can accomplish. Barbara Jordan had a charismatic presence. She was the only black woman from a southern state to serve in the United States Congress (1973–1979), the first black to hold a seat in the Texas Senate, the first black keynote speaker at a national convention of the Democratic party, and she was a leader of the Civil Rights movement. If she had not been stricken with multiple sclerosis, this lady probably would have been seated on the Supreme Court. She overcame obstacles when racism was very prevalent in the United States. Racism continues to manifest itself in these United States. Her attendance at the Boston Law School was no picnic. She attended school in Boston during the years when Boston was not a friendly place toward blacks. Barbara was born and raised in Texas, and she made this statement to a National Geographic reporter in 1989: "I get from the soil and spirit of Texas the feeling that I, as an individual, can accomplish whatever I want to, and that there are no limits, that you can just keep going, just keep soaring. I like that spirit," (utexas.edu/know, 02/18/13).

You, too, can have the drive these women have displayed. Do not concentrate on societal ills; instead, concentrate on the productive and positive things in life and, like these women, run the race that is in place before you. You should not be confined to a particular profession because you are a female and black. Do not entertain the idea that black women are not to perform in a certain profession, or that you are not smart enough to head an organization; don't be afraid to show that there is a place for you in any endeavor you wish to become involved. If there is a desire and call to preach the gospel, go and preach. If you have the desire to be a doctor, go and prepare to be a doctor. The arena is vast. Just know what you want, ask God to help you get it, and go get it.

Program Your Mind with Good Thoughts

Have you programmed your mind with good thoughts, or do you have problems with impure thoughts? If you don't program your mind with good and wholesome thoughts, you may find yourself speaking and acting in ineffectual ways. When programming your mind, you can review this passage, "Whatsoever things are true, whatsoever things are honest, whatsoever things are just, whatsoever things are pure, whatsoever things are lovely, whatsoever things are of good report; if there be any virtue, and if there be any praise, think on these things" (Philippians 4:8, KJV). In this passage of scripture, Paul reminds us to program our minds with good thoughts. Examine what you allow into your mind by striving to focus on pleasing and pleasant things. You will then find that wholesome things flow from your mouth when you speak.

If it is difficult to have positive and wholesome things flowing from you, ask God for a cleansing of the mind. There are other things you can do to cleanse the mind. Here are some suggestions:

1. **Learn to deal with anger: Decrease what you get angry about. Anger can place your life in disarray. Be concerned**

about things that go wrong. Do not allow them to devastate you. Remember: this, too, shall pass.

2. Look for good in each person: Realize that each person has been through experiences that makes them different or may cause them to be or act contrary to what you believe. Look at people with love and understanding while praying for them. Believe there is some good in everyone.

3. Remember to forgive: Just remember to forgive those who trespass against you, and your heavenly Father will forgive you.

4. Make every effort to have good moods: Life has many ups and downs. Sometimes it feels like the whole world is in a complete mess, and you can become depressed. If this becomes a long-term state of being, by all means, seek professional help. However, if this is just a short-term phase, stop and think about the good things in life. Surround yourself with encouraging people. You don't need to be surrounded by negative people.

5. Do mood-changing activities: Have you ever felt as though your mood or frame of mind is holding you back and preventing you from moving forward in life? Discover what you enjoy doing and what comforts you, then take time to indulge in those activities. I find comfort in these things: listening to lively music, looking at previous vacation pictures, walking and observing the wonders of nature, and travelling. I find hope and beauty in many things. What a pleasure it is to walk along the waters' edge or just sit and watch the beauty of nature. Magnificently, the sun rises in the east and slips away beneath the western horizon at the end of each day. That gives me a glorious feeling. Like ancient man, I marvel at the beauty of the night sky, with the fullness of the moon and the twinkling of the stars that light up the night, knowing that there must be a God somewhere. To hear the birds as they chirp in the swaying trees is exhilarating and mood changing for me.

It is wonderful to watch the birds as they take flight in an amazing display of grace, mercy, and beauty. Then there is the smell of flowers and their beautiful colors. I like to refer to the flowers as the Master's bouquet. These things help me know that my God is truly at work in his universe. I enjoy lying back, allowing my body to go limp, closing my eyes, and taking deep breaths, inhaling and exhaling slowly while thinking of nothing. It relaxes my mind and renews my spirit. These things help me to focus on a positive mind-set. I love to travel and observe the beauty of other lands and people. I recently met a young man in Jamaica. He said to me, "I am the Jamaican king of fire eating. I love to dance." As he danced and talked about his passion for fire eating, his face beamed with an unbelievable smile. I thought, at that moment in time, I was listening to one of the happiest people on earth. I was so inspired by this young man with a marvelous personality. Exploring other lands and their cultures can give you joy. Please do not forget to enjoy and appreciate the life and opportunities that you have in your own land. I have a fondness for great Gospel, Hawaiian and Caribbean music; I can sit and listen for hours. While you are involved in great activities that you enjoy, consciously avoid negative thoughts. It is a blessing to behold wonderful things. Participation in activities that you enjoy can relax you, while placing you in a position to become a person who sees new possibilities. And remember: sharing laughter and talking with others can provide the aura that will help you maintain positive feelings. It's up to you and your preference.

Remove Negative Thinking

Are you having difficulty controlling negative thoughts? All of us have times when we are confronted by unfavorable thoughts. It is a pretty common human trait. After you read this section, I hope you will be able to recognize what negative thinking is and be ready to end your negative thinking. Keep this in mind: Change your mind and you will elevate yourself to new heights. Positive thoughts will allow you to soar to new heights, mastering the goal you have in mind. Keep a positive and healthy attitude, and you will experience happiness and an abundant life. Proverbs 23:7 says, "For as he thinketh in his heart, so is he," (KJV). Keep an attitude that is positive, then see yourself rise to the position you wish to attain. This principle is demonstrated throughout the Bible.

Negativism is characterized by bad attitude, complaining, doubt and resistance. It is common to find negative people disapproving and complaining about other people and situations.

Sometimes, we find ourselves surrounded by negative relatives and friends. They complain about everything: other siblings, hard times, aches and pains, jobs, wayward children, and even their spouses. We hear the same complaints from generation to generation. Some people look at things just to see if they can find something wrong. Negativism can dominate your life and keep you in a constant state of unhappiness. Negativism produces undesirable thoughts and unenthusiastic people. If that sort of existence is prolonged, you could become comfortable in the midst of misery and strife. Would this be good for you? One young minister had an elderly aunt in his family. She would call him on Sunday mornings before sermon time to share her thoughts. She complained and talked about relatives, acquaintances, and him. She was so disapproving that she criticized people who died many years prior. He finally had to stop accepting her calls because he carried the negative thoughts into the pulpit. Do not surround yourself with negative people, and do not listen to destructive comments. People who are negative will drag others down with them. They are unhappy and will make others unhappy. This principle ties in with the old saying that "misery loves company."

If a goal becomes so overwhelming that it causes you to think negatively, then plan to take actions to achieve smaller goals that will lead to the accomplishment of the larger goal. Visualize yourself with the results you hope to achieve. Stay away from negative people who discourage you. Do not allow yourself to become stuck in negative thinking. It devastates and keeps you from accomplishing anything. It destroys; it does not build. You can lose sight of your visions, dreams, plans, and actions. When stuck in the negative mode, you can miss opportunities when they come.

One of the most important aspects of life is to be able to look back on a life well spent and see that you maintained a positive outlook about yourself, the things around you, and others. Negative thoughts and deeds can be draining to you and the people you come in contact with. The following suggestions will aid in doing away with negative thinking:

1. **Be aware of your negative thoughts: Are you a person with negative thoughts and a bad attitude? Do you know people like this? You must be able to recognize that there is negative thinking present. Some people complain and think ill about themselves and others, but they are not conscious of what they are doing. When bad thoughts occur, change to something positive so that you can be a dynamic and fruitful individual. Negative thoughts will keep you unhappy and cause you to feel inadequate. Be careful about saying things like "I'm tired," "I'm having a bad day," or "I'm not smart enough to compete." Statements like these are self-defeating. Instead, try saying "I am blessed and highly favored by God and good things shall always accompany me." Remember, thoughts can become a reality. Life becomes better when you change your mode of thinking. Ask God to help you to always have positive thoughts.**

2. **Surround yourself with confident and positive-thinking people: Do you think the people you associate with have an effect on how you achieve or how you live your life? As a pastor and teacher, I have observed that people who hang together are doing the same things. The students who behave and get good grades surround themselves with students who have the same behavior and academic achievements. I have also**

observed that people who do drugs and are dysfunctional in other ways associate with people who do as they do. One of my senior students, whom I will refer to as Gary, admitted to me that he was once a hall walker. He skipped classes, he was constantly getting into trouble, and he had no interest in academics. Now Gary is not hanging out with the old crowd; he is a Christian, and he aspires to attend seminary to become a minister. His grades have improved tremendously. He helps keep order in the classroom by embarrassing students for disrespecting the teacher. In life, there are toxic people and there are those who nurture. Toxic people kill dreams. They discourage. On the other hand, people who nurture are positive, constructive, and supportive. They make you feel great about yourself and what you are doing. When you have a dream and a planned goal, stay away from people who focus on what you can't do. It can be depressing when you are told you are not capable of achieving something. Don't allow anyone to discourage you by breaking your spirit; remain determined to press toward your goals.

3. Feel good about yourself and draw others to you: Fifty percent of the women I surveyed agreed that associating with positive people made them feel good about themselves. It also helped them draw others into a congenial group because people want to be around other positive people. You will find that when you give support to another person, it will be reciprocated in this sort of gathering. It feels good seeing upbeat, positive, and smiling people on Sunday mornings as I make that climb to the pulpit. It is a blessing.

4. Speak encouraging words: How are you accustomed to talking to people? Are you the one who is spewing negative words or spreading rumors? Proverbs 15:1 says, "A soft answer turneth away wrath; but grievous words stir up anger," (KJV). When your thoughts are positive, you will speak in positive terms and avoid unforgiving words.

5. **Do not pass judgment on others:** Do you sometimes find yourself speaking ill of others or being judgmental? Let us remember: all of us have faults and sometimes our behavior is not acceptable to others. Do not allow yourself to be critical of others. The judging of people will come at a later time by a higher being. 1 Corinthians 4:5 says,

    "Therefore judge nothing before the time, until the Lord come, who both will bring to light the hidden things of darkness, and will make manifest the counsels of the hearts: and then shall every man have praise of God," (KJV).

    Always speak well of others and speak well to others. Paul advises us: "Let no corrupt communication proceed out of your mouth, but that which is good to the use of edifying, that it may minister grace unto the hearers," (Ephesians 4:29, KJV). God wants us to speak words of encouragement to one another. Help others feel good about themselves by saying something positive to them. For example, say, "You are a fantastic artist" or "You are a great speaker!" Remember that words have a tremendous impact. You will be surprised by the power of positive language. The Bible teaches that "death and life are in the power of the tongue," (Proverbs 18:21, KJV). Be careful what you say. You can always speak positively to others if you remember to do away with undesirable words and phrases. Instead of saying "the glass is half empty," say "the glass is half full." Practice leaving words and phrases like "not," "I can't," "I hate," and "I don't" out of your vocabulary. Instead of focusing on expressing what you do not want, focus on expressing what you do want. I must confess that all of my life I have been troubled by the phrase "I cannot." Early in life, I removed "I cannot" from my vocabulary. I do not permit my children to use the phrase. I want them to know that all things are

possible, and you can do anything you put in your mind. I want to instill in them that all obstacles can be overcome. It only takes hard work, determination, and an unwavering faith in God. Your dreams are attainable, so have big dreams! I had to let my children know that their goals are only accomplished if they work hard and allow God to work with them. Matthew 20:26 says, "With God all things are possible," (KJV). The power to achieve does not rest in our hands, but with God. Lean and depend on him.

Go on, be a dreamer and dream the impossible dream! Look at President Obama, who said, "I can." The president of these United States dared to dream and believe that anything is possible. We never thought a black man would become president of these United States in our lifetime. As you focus on being positive, it is good to be grateful and give thanks. Remember not to focus on the negative and unpleasant things in your life. Take pleasure in the pleasant things of life and do not constantly complain. Instead, think about those wonderful things that have already happened in your life. Focus on the great things you have instead of dwelling on things you do not have. Think about how wonderful it is to see the beginning of a brand new day. You are still on this wonderful earth that God created just for you. Be thankful, for many have gone on into eternity. You are still among the living, and you can accomplish the desires of your heart. Keep up your positive thinking.

Chapter 2

Self-Confidence is Key

Are you a confident black woman or are you lacking self-esteem? My survey of 200 black women revealed that more than half of the women surveyed felt inadequate about something, whether it was their appearance or their ability to accomplish difficult tasks. Just think of how wonderful it is to feel good about your abilities, accomplishments, and appearance.

Your physical appearance, personality, or social skills may not be up to par or what you think they should be. If you need to improve on your social skills, practice, take tips from others who have the skills you admire, or read up on some social skill tips. Mostly, just exhibit your natural self, and your social skills will sharpen over time. Personality is personal, which means you must be the genuine you. You do have a bright side, so just display it! You may look in the mirror and decide you'd like to tweak your appearance—that's okay. A fresh face with a dab of makeup can, if you so choose, change your appearance to a different look that you'd like to display at times. You can tweak your look with practice right in front of the mirror; try different makeup applications until you get the look that suits you. You may even get a friend who is makeup savvy to help you tweak your naturally beautiful look. Just remember, you are simply trying to reach an increased sense of self-confidence, not preparing for a photo shoot.

Some darker skinned women expressed that they did not feel as attractive as lighter skinned women, according to my survey results. They associated attractiveness with lighter skin. They have allowed themselves to succumb to the media's portrayal of beauty, which usually spotlights women with lighter complexions. If a darker skinned woman is used, it is usually a shorter shot. Additionally, the number of darker skinned women included is usually a minimized sampling with a deliberate, paced appearance. Of course, when you pick up a magazine that is dedicated to women of color, you will see images of the darker skinned black woman. But this is not mass media because these magazines are usually purchased by us. Should this then determine that you are not beautiful? Of course not! Complexion does not guarantee or determine beauty. Beauty is the uniqueness of the individual, so never wish to look like someone else; realize that each of us is unique in our own beauty, and we are beauty to behold.

There are women who feel that being overweight makes them less attractive to men. That cannot be true because there are indeed men who love more bountiful women! Someone once said, "It is not who you think you are that holds you back, it is who you think you are not." This is a true saying. Your skin color and your body size are a part of who you are. These are the beautiful elements of you. If you desire to lose weight, perhaps for health reasons or to tone up your body muscle, it's okay. Some medications can cause weight gain or weight loss, but they are keeping you healthy, so you must learn to love your image. Your body weight is still your unique makeup. Our skin color has delivered us as the combination of our parents and our ancestors, which means it is our very own unique beauty trait. When you are self-confident, you are able to embrace all that you are composed of and appreciate it. This is what it means to love all that is you.

A long time ago (it seems like another life), I was shy, timid, and would frequently cry about things that I had no control over. I remember it was my first day of registration at the university. The registration at this school was so unorganized, and I was sent from one place to another all day without being able to register. I went home frustrated and ready to give up on going to college. However, my husband returned with me and walked me through the whole process. He was emphatic about staff members giving good directions and not sending me from one place to another. He made sure that the tasks for registration were accomplished. From that day forward, I began to take on challenges and obstacles that confronted me. I began to realize that I am not insignificant. I am a child of God. I am important and I will be heard. I learned not to allow obstacles to alter my plans. I have learned to persevere through peaks and valleys because I know that God continues to bring me through the trials and tribulations of life. I have developed an astonishing faith that lets me know that I am special, unique, wonderful, and creative in God's sight. He has great things in store for you and me. I am a child of the King and a strong black woman in Christ. I believe "I can do all things through Christ which strengtheneth me," (Philippians 4:13, KJV). Are you a self-confident person, or do you lack the self-confidence to make things better on your own?

Do not lose your self-confidence based on others' opinions of you. They do not have control over how you feel or perform. Do not pattern yourself after other people, and do not depend on others to decide what should be done in your life. Suggestions are okay if you seek them, but the ultimate determinations should be yours. Just have a passion for what you are striving to do in life. When you are excited about what you are doing, you will certainly enjoy it. Think for yourself and know that your undertakings are to be done right because they are a reflection of you.

Is it possible to face the challenges that confront you in life? It sure is. First, do not be timid, shy, or fearful. Goals can be accomplished. If in doubt, take Jesus along with you. Focus on training yourself to believe that your goals can be accomplished. It is all about transforming your mind to believe that you can and will do what you set out to do. Look at women like Tina Turner, Halle Berry, Alicia Keys, and others who have succeeded in spite of obstacles.

Many times, obstacles will get in the way of what you are doing. Ladies, believe me, life is going to throw you some big problems. Don't allow these stumbling blocks to ground or deter your plans. God gives us the power to overcome obstacles in life. Sometimes we allow difficulties, challenges, or adversities to control our lives because of doubts and fears. Fear can be devastating to one's self-confidence, for it is the scoundrel that hides a range of feelings. Fear is a hostile force that God is willing to replace with comfort. John 14:27 says, "Peace I leave with you, my peace I give unto you: not as the world giveth, give I unto you. Let not your heart be troubled, neither let it be afraid," (KJV). Remember to pray: "Dear Lord, I am overwhelmed by this feeling of fear. Take these worries, obstacles, and blocks; move them, O Lord, and free my mind of stress, anxiety, and fear. Instill in me the will to proceed toward the goal at hand. Thank you." Your pastor can be a helpful resource when you are afraid.

Fear is devastating to self-control, self-confidence, relationships, and health. Get rid of fear. The Bible says, "Be careful for nothing; but in everything, by prayer and supplication with thanksgiving let your requests be made known unto God. And the peace of God, which passeth all understanding, shall keep your hearts and minds through Christ Jesus," (Philippians 4:6–7, KJV). Enrich your prayer life. If you are fearful about your endeavors, pray a little bit more. Maybe God has allowed obstacles or challenges into our lives (mean people, insurmountable problems, and difficult situations) so that we will have faith in Him.

Believe me, all of us shall face doubts, concerns, challenges, disappointments, sorrows, and failures. Failure is embarrassing, but get up, brush off, and begin again. It was Theodore Roosevelt who said, "The only man who never makes a mistake is a man who never does anything." Some mistakes are going to be made, but be an explorer of life, and those mistakes will only make you stronger and a better person. Remember that mistakes serve as great learning experiences and tremendous stepping stones. If you make a mistake, then depend on God for guidance. It just makes good sense to follow God because he gives us hope and courage in difficult situations. Continuously say to yourself, "With God's help, I will do this, for he is with me always."

Take a look at these Biblical characters that faced obstacles and failure: There was Peter, who denied Christ; Paul persecuted Christians; David committed murder to conceal adultery; and Joseph was sold into slavery by his own brothers. Each one of these Biblical characters was blessed to fulfill God's purpose for them. Do not allow failure to discourage you.

After enduring work in the cotton fields and the extreme heat under the midday sun in the flatlands of Texas years ago, I knew I could excel at anything. The Bible tells us, "In all thy ways acknowledge him, and he shall direct thy path" (Proverbs 3:6, KJV). I knew that I was to acknowledge God in all that I did. In spite of hardships and no money, I embarked upon a journey that included college. I had no idea how I would realize my dream to be educated and working in a field that I enjoyed. As a child I was taught to always pray and have faith in God. I kept the faith, and I believe it was by the grace of God that I landed a job that I retired from after thirty years. My first manager allowed me to report late to work after attending class every day. After enjoying a career in banking, I went on to teach in the public schools and pastor a church. I placed God first in my life and I continue to look to him for everything.

Make him a part of your dreams, values, and goals. Trust him in every choice. Your self-confidence comes from God's guidance. Consult him persistently; you are not the wise and smart one, he is. Nothing can be done without him. You have no reason to feel inadequate. The following tips will help to enhance your self-confidence:

1. **Believe in yourself: Do you believe you can be a success by setting goals and achieving them, or do you always make excuses about why you can't achieve what you want? It is time to change those thoughts. It is necessary to believe that you can and will achieve what you desire. Make the necessary changes in your life to make the best of it. Instead of thinking up excuses about why it is impossible to succeed in life, recite phrases to yourself, such as "I can do this," "I will succeed," and "I can succeed." Set goals, lay out plans and follow them. Never say "I cannot" because this never accomplishes anything. Develop belief in yourself, and this will establish the prospect of a favorable outcome. Continue**

to build up your self-confidence; it is in the mind that success is identified and attained. When you accomplish a difficult deed, pat yourself on the back and celebrate your victory! That's a "feel good" moment that boosts your self-esteem. The mind is a powerful instrument to use for self-improvement; therefore, believe in yourself. There is no need to feel inferior or incapable.

2. **Inferiority complex has no place:** Do you have an inferiority complex? Do you feel uncomfortable or intimidated when in front of new people? Do you feel that sometimes people will see you as stupid, incompetent, or incapable? You are not alone in these feelings. I remember feeling inferior and not having the courage to stand before people and speak. However, I constantly prayed, asking God to remove my fear of speaking before people because it was preventing me from succeeding. I felt that God made a call upon my life to preach the gospel, and I wanted to do great things for the Lord. I remembered Moses, too, felt inadequate and lacked self-confidence when God commanded him to go into Egypt and tell pharaoh to, "Let my people go." God promised to be with Moses as he went forth into Egypt. Therefore, Moses stepped forth in confidence. God was with Moses, and he is with us. That lets me know that we can step out on faith because God promises us his resources just as he promised Moses.

Do not compare yourself with other women. Their accomplishments are their very own and do not impact your life and accomplishments. The Bible tells us that the children of Israel experienced an inferiority complex after the twelve spies came back from exploring the promised land. The spies said, "And there we saw the giants, the sons of A'nak, which come of the giants; and we were in our own sight as grasshoppers, and so we were in their sight," (Numbers 13:33, KJV). Hold your head up and walk with confidence. Act with confidence even if you do not feel confident. Reading about other successful women of color may also help. Get together with a friend who encourages you or have lunch with a successful person. Ask questions and ask for suggestions about your own life goals and how to achieve them. Sit down and list the things you have done well in your life. You have know-how, and you have achieved accomplishments which you feel good about. Isn't it wonderful to realize that there are countless experiences under your belt? God has given all of us special gifts. Ask him for instructions on how to use them in extraordinary ways. It would help to get rid of that inferiority complex by saying, "I am such a wonderful speaker," or "I am a great teacher," etc. You will see a change in your behavior and the way you see yourself. Be persistent in affirming and encouraging yourself. Have faith in yourself and know that you are that self-confident person with dreams and the endurance to accomplish outstanding goals. Focus on the following:

1. **Love yourself: Do you love yourself? Loving yourself is a prerequisite for possessing self-confidence. When you love yourself, confidence grows. Some ladies feel that a romantic relationship can alleviate feelings of emptiness, and that it will provide the sense of fulfillment and happiness they desire. That may happen, but it will only be temporary if you do not love yourself. A meaningful romantic relationship is not a substitute for the love you must feel for yourself. When you don't feel good about yourself, you are apt to have low self-esteem, which can be detrimental. It certainly can interfere with your aspirations. Lucille Ball said, "Love yourself first, and everything falls into line. You really have to love yourself to get anything done in this world" (American radio and motion-picture actress and comedy star, 1911–1989) quotationspage.com/quote/31062html). Work on developing self-love. Start by not being so hard on yourself: welcome compliments, take care of your health needs, pamper yourself, praise yourself, think positively about yourself, celebrate your achievements, and do not judge yourself harshly for failure. Sometimes you can be your own worst faultfinder, which is not productive. No human**

being is unflawed; recognize and accept imperfection. Just don't ever forget to love yourself!

2. **Trust in yourself: Know that dreams can become realities. God said to Joshua, "There shall not any man be able to stand before thee all the days of thy life; as I was with Moses, so I will be with thee; I will not fail thee, nor forsake thee," (Joshua 1:5, KJV). With each great endeavor comes challenges. Without God, challenges can frighten you, slow you down, and, in some cases, hold you back. But trusting in God allows you to trust yourself. God promises to be with you, to direct your paths, and to sustain you.**

I was so impressed by a story I read in *Time Magazine* about a woman, Alysa Stanton, who was ordained as the first black, female rabbi. Before she was ordained by Hebrew Union College, she faced hardships and jumped over hurdles. She faced rejection from Jews and Christians alike. She stood her ground and spoke out about what she believed and realized her dream (time.com/time/nation/article/0,8599,190324500html, (June 6, 2009). Do as she did. Be clear and speak out about what you believe in. Don't forget to stick up for yourself when others are being obnoxious and voicing their opinion against what you feel is the right goal for you. Trust yourself to do these things. With God, all things are possible. He gives us the strength to make dreams a reality.

3. **Develop breathtaking self-esteem: How is your self-esteem? Is it low? If your self-esteem is low and unhealthy, fix that. Be vigilant when discussing your goals with others, and refuse to listen to people who focus on what you cannot do or what you do not have the ability to do. When you realize and accept that you have the knowledge, skills, and willingness to learn as well as the strong desire to do something, learn to listen to your own assessment and rely on its validity. The lack of others' approval should never deter your determination. God has given you what you need to succeed in life.**

Something as small as the way you sit or stand can show that you possess self-esteem. Show that you are competent and not intimidated. Don't slouch or slump when you sit or stand. Hold your head up high when you walk and talk. Make eye contact with the person you are communicating with. A pleasant smile is comforting to others, and it brings you a feeling of composure. Straighten your back, square your shoulders, and keep your arms unfolded. Show that you are alert and interested in your surroundings at all times. Be able to state your goals and anything else you have to say in direct and certain terms. Never resort to blaming others when outcomes are less than what is desired, but persevere and plan another route to your goal.

4. **Develop independence: Do you find yourself depending on your parents, siblings, spouses, children, friends, or any others? Remove the handicap. It is time to sprout wings and fly on your own. Many times we find ourselves too dependent on others, especially when they have always provided our bare necessities in life. What you must realize is that when you continue to lean on people beyond adulthood, even when the assistance continues, those people may stop being your crutch, maybe even abruptly. This may happen because they no longer wish to assist you, they are no longer in the position to assist, or they could die, leaving you to fend for yourself when you don't know how. That can be devastating. Even in the case of losing a spouse, you should be in the position to sustain yourself, whether through plans made with the spouse and/or the security you have built for yourself. Ladies, remember that the only constant in life is God, so we must lean and depend on him.**

Even in an intimate relationship, there should be a healthy amount of independence. Each person should have a certain amount of freedom. One partner may need a certain amount of quiet time spent alone without the other feeling as if they are being slighted or neglected. Treat yourself to some personal time away from family and friends.

Do something for yourself that is enjoyable. My husband, John, and I, before his death, knew how to spend quiet time away from each other. I spent hours fishing, which was boring for him. John enjoyed his alone time playing pool, gardening, and driving around the countryside. I love to go on cruises, and he hated ships, so we arranged to do things that we liked independently. He often travelled home to North Carolina alone. A sense of independence does not weaken a relationship, but strengthens it. We were very secure in our relationship. We had a wonderful relationship, which he marveled about on his death bed. The times we spent together are truly missed. When you don't create solitary moments of content for yourself, the loss of a mate and other life changes can become even more difficult to accept. A sense of independence allows you to be able to accept the things you cannot change.

5. **Speak success to yourself: Talk to yourself and affirm yourself. Say to yourself, "I am an achiever," "I love myself," "I can lose weight or gain weight and be healthy," "I am beautiful," "I am a success," or "I will be successful." Continuously tell yourself positive affirmations like those previously mentioned, and they will become a reality.**

6. **All things are possible: Sometimes goals seem out of reach and unattainable. Do not allow anything to prevent you from indulging in believing that all things are possible. With God, you can accomplish your goal. Do not use the word "impossible." Set goals and begin to have huge thoughts and great expectations; it is possible, and it will happen. You can succeed in your endeavors, even if you are having difficulty with determining how to get important tasks done. You will figure it out. Remember: God is your strength, and call upon him when you feel that you cannot go any further. Isaiah 40:31 says, "But they that wait upon the Lord shall renew their strength; they shall mount up with wings as eagles; they shall run, and not be weary; and they shall walk, and not faint," (KJV). When we wait upon the Lord, we expect that he will give us the strength that**

he promises. **Do not walk around thinking that you will not accomplish your goal. Say to yourself, "I need to set a deadline for the accomplishment of this goal." A goal's deadline is good so that one will not procrastinate and never accomplish the goal. I suggest that you set a timeline for smaller goals that will help you work toward the larger goal. As you work you can see progress and meet that final deadline.**

7. **Learn from failure: How do you view failure? Many times, we women are confronted and defeated by life's difficulties; sometimes, we are overwhelmed and devastated because we have been jerked around. Some fall and stay down, and some get up. Getting up is done through the power that God gives us if we have faith in him. Do not avoid getting involved in what you desire in life because you are afraid of failure or are afraid of what people will say or think about you. The Bible says, "If God be for us, who can be against us, (Romans, 8:31, KJV)?" Repeat this over and over to yourself, and your fear will be alleviated. Remember that problems, obstacles, and failures are going to occur. Again, failure is a part of life that is normal and becomes part of a valuable learning experience. Failure alerts the mind to devise another plan and to be persistent in pursuing a goal. It is always painful to fail. Acceptance eases the pain.**

One of President Jimmy Carter's famous quotes is: "But it's better to fail while striving for something wonderful, challenging, adventurous, and uncertain than to say, 'I don't want to try, because I may not succeed completely."[2] Failures teach us to handle the situation the second time around. They often give us new direction and the strength to endure and succeed. I can testify that there are lessons in failure. I mention one failure here. I learned to alter my goal after I failed to

---

2 Jimmy Carter "Sources of Strength: Meditations on Scripture for a Living Faith. (U.S.A.: Times Books, October,1999), 240.

accomplish the goal of being an administrator at a prison for women. Early in life I thought that I could help someone to steer their life in the right direction, by heading up a prison for women. That goal was not accomplished, but I got a new sense of direction. There have been other failures and I know how things should not be done. Failure has had a humbling effect on my life, and it certainly has let me know that we fail because we are human. I have learned to embrace failures, and, hopefully, I can allow my life to touch other lives as they deal with their trials. Make realistic goals. Believe in yourself, and do your best. Believe in yourself and what you are doing, and success will happen. I believe Ralph Waldo Emerson said it best: "Our greatest glory is not in never failing but in rising up every time we fail" (Poet, Lecturer and Essayist, 1803–1882).

8. **Don't worry: Do you constantly worry and find yourself stressed out over certain situations that confront you? Worrying comes about because of anxiety, fear, or some other vague threat. Worrying is an experience that all human beings have. Please do not misunderstand me. Realistically deal with real and true problems in your life. Human beings cannot ignore risks. However, it does help to submit those difficulties to God in prayer and not allow them to cripple or immobilize you. Some people have the tendency to worry about every little thing: grades in school, job performance, disease, financial problems, children, spouses, and the like. Dr. Charles Mayo of the famous Mayo Clinic says, "There's a growing mountain of evidence to suggest that worry is the chief contributor to depression, nervous breakdowns, high blood pressure, heart attacks, and early death. Stress kills. I've never known a man to die from hard work, but I've known a lot who died from worry" (The Ziglar Weekly Newsletter, Weekly News, Motivation, and Fun Content, June 30, 2009 edition, Zig on Why Worry by Zig Ziglar). Worrying can cause you to be sick, miserable, and unable to function at all. It can also render you as unfriendly and**

may even affect your ability to trust in God. Worry will immobilize you so much so that it will not allow the oomph to fight against what causes the worry. Someone once said, "Worry is like a rocking chair. It will give you something to do, but it won't get you anywhere." Set goals and plan for tomorrow, but don't worry about anything; it is a waste of time. Do not resort to alcohol and other drugs to cope with worry, fear, or anxiety. They do not get rid of the problems we face; they will only intensify the problems. The key is to set goals and plan well. A relationship with God changes these pointless worries into spiritual productivity and purpose.

When it comes to worrying, I have concluded that it is useless. I believe in taking one day at a time. Why should we worry about yesterday? It is gone. Why should we worry about tomorrow? It may never come. Relax and be concerned about today.

9. **Don't blame others: Are you guilty of blaming others when unpleasant things happen in your life? Do not allow yourself to blame others for your short comings. An example of this would be to say, "My parents taught me nothing about being successful" or "If it had not been for my mother, my father, or my brother, I would have gone to college."**

I know a woman, whom I will refer to as Gloria. She has a drug problem, but blames her mother's inappropriate behavior for her problems. Her mother was addicted to drugs and died of a drug overdose. Gloria has to take the responsibility for her association with the wrong people and getting involved in the drug culture. Gloria made the wrong decisions and failed to be all that God wanted her to be. Gloria did not make the effort to enjoy the great possibilities that life has to offer. The mother cannot be blamed because Gloria has not made an attempt to overcome her own weaknesses that keep her overwhelmed, causing her to continue to use drugs. I am truly saddened by Gloria's plight, for she is suffering from the Acquired Immune Deficiency Syndrome. Blaming others is not a way of accepting responsibility for your own actions. Do not make excuses for not making progress. When something goes wrong in your life, remember that your life story is written by you. Your destiny lies in your hands and only your hands. If we become helpless or lethargic in controlling bad situations in our lives, we cannot blame others. No one can influence what happens in your life unless you allow yourself to be influenced. God has empowered you with the tremendous power to create vision and accomplish goals. You have to make the right decisions in any given situation or circumstance. You have the power. Accusing others for your lack of progress will keep you trapped in an unproductive situation. Realize that the individuals you are blaming for your failures are mere mortals on this journey of life, and they may not want to do what it takes to be successful. They may fall short of what is proper living in the sight of God and society. They, too, have been endowed with free will. Decisions are our own. Take responsibility for your life; make good decisions, and enjoy the fullness of life.

10. **Gain a sense of success: Are you a successful person? You are a successful person when you are in a position that you are comfortable and satisfied with. Ladies, your mind is the most dynamic force you possess. Allow your mind to focus and believe in extraordinary achievements, and possibilities will become realities. Believe it, and achieve it. Not only believe that success will come, but act like it. Talk to people who have been successful. Ask them about their pursuits, and the obstacles they had to overcome to get to the place where they are. Many have overcome obstacles that you cannot begin to imagine. Henry David Thoreau said, "Go confidently into the direction of your dreams! Live the life you've imagined. As you simplify your life, the laws of the universe will be simpler," (Retrieved from http://www. microgiving.com/profile/423161   p://www.microgiving. com/profile/423161).**
11. **Take risks: Every day we take risks in life, and plans do not**

always come out as charted. Live your life with confidence. You cannot live your life in fear that something will go wrong. In the book of Ecclesiastes, Solomon indicates that life involves risk and opportunity. Just because there are no guarantees in life, we do not have to resolve to do nothing, nor should we be sad. We are to face the risks and challenges of life with God's direction and faith.

Ecclesiastes 11:1–6 says,

"Cast thy bread upon the waters: for thou shalt find it after many days. Give a portion to seven, and also to eight; for thou knowest not what evil shall be upon the earth. If the clouds be full of rain, they empty themselves upon the earth: and if the tree fall toward the south, or toward the north, in the place where the tree falleth, there it shall be. He that observeth the wind shall not sow; and he that regardeth the clouds shall not reap. As thou knowest not what is the way of the spirit, nor how the bones do grow in the womb of her that is with child: even so thou knowest not the works of God who maketh all. In the morning sow thy seed, and in the evening withhold not thine hand: for thou knowest not whether shall prosper, either this or that, or whether they both shall be alike good," (KJV).

Solomon encourages risks, for the right time may never come for you to start working on that dream. Do not wait for conditions to change; they may never change. Get started living life to the fullest. As Solomon teaches, take risks, for nothing ventured means nothing gained. There is no better time to step out on faith than right now.

12. **Keep jealousy in check: Do you struggle with jealousy? Do you resent women whom you think are successful because you believe that you could never be that successful? How many times is a woman looked at and envied because it just looked like she was on top of the world—nice clothes,**

beautiful home, and a not-so-bad-looking man? We have a tendency to develop a strong desire to acquire material things. The more we have, the more we feel that we look successful in our society. What we must know is that material possessions do not bring genuine happiness. Let's be realistic: jealousy is not an emotion you can afford. It evolves from a lack of self-confidence. Do not worry about what someone else is doing, or where they are going, or what they might accomplish. Competition is a part of our lives; therefore, jealousy is engrained in the fabric of our society. All human beings are prone to jealousy.

Jealousy gives one the tendency to make negative comments about people. It is important to realize that another person's progress or success will not hinder what another can accomplish or is capable of doing in life. Lives are to be patterned after Jesus Christ and no one else. Let us continue to look at him. Remember: the Apostle Paul says that the important things are the things that we cannot see, like truth, compassion, justice, service, and love. Instead of being jealous, it would be wonderful to develop relationships with people where it is comfortable to be happy for their achievements. Peace comes when we stop wishing or attempting to commandeer more than someone else. There is a struggle in our society to possess bigger and better things than another person. It is more advantageous to ask, "What can I do to live a better life in the eyes of my Savior?" Do you want to be delivered from a jealous heart? Ask God to help you share the joys and achievement of others that you know. Ask him not to allow you to destroy wholesome relationships by being jealous. Pray that you establish self-confidence and self-esteem within yourself to help you feel great about yourself. In light of this, you will attract friends that will want to be in your company forever. Jealousy does not keep people around, but pushes them away.

We find ourselves being jealous in our love relationships. Maybe this is because of the fear that we may lose our mate, and this fear is devastating. Some of the women interviewed admitted being jealous of some man because someone else was interested in him. Jealousy will not allow you to hang on to anyone; jealousy will definitely cause a person to run away from you. And sometimes, jealousy makes you perceive something that is not present. You would do well to create your own wonderful place in this world, be thankful for what you now possess, and ask God for blessed characteristics that all individuals need: understanding, patience, wisdom, and compassion. Please ask him for that all-important peace of mind. These virtues can be accomplished if we only believe in the power of God. It is not always about who has the biggest house, best car, and the most money. It is not always about skin color. Sometimes we can be insecure in many areas. Sometimes we can be unforgiving, but it is most important to learn to support one another in our endeavors. Celebrate the success of other black women, and never allow yourself to be threatened by the accomplishments and successes of others. Stop self-hatred by celebrating who you are, and be thankful for how God has made you.

Chapter 3

You Are a Beautiful Black Woman

Are you a beautiful black woman? Yes, you are a magnificent and beautiful person with much to offer. One of the most noteworthy things about God's creation is that it is unique and beautiful. He loves his creations and refuses to let them feel any other way but beautiful. All human beings are magnificent creatures, and God wants everyone to be positive thinking, self-confident, and beautiful. If this is not the case, the mind has to be opened to God's love. He will change the perception of an individual. He will change how you see yourself and make you a brand new woman.

Are you a woman that spends time in self-criticism about how you look? As mentioned earlier, my survey revealed that many of the dark skinned black women felt that they were not as attractive as the lighter skinned black women because of their darker color. Some mentioned that they thought that light skin, huge butts, big chests, and thin lips had a lot to do with being beautiful. They believe that women with these attributes are more attractive to men. This idea has been passed down through generations, and some black men help to perpetuate this thinking. Some black men in our society state a preference for lighter skinned women. Do not be deceived ladies. Light skinned ladies get played by men as much as the dark skinned ladies.

It is hard for some of our black teenagers and young black women because the media constantly portrays white as being beautiful. Our society and the world have come to regard the European standard for beauty, which is light skin, thin lips, thin nose, and straight hair, as standard; therefore, it is hard for some of our black women to feel good about their natural appearance. Beauty is so diverse that no particular characteristic personifies it. Have we regressed in our culture to a time when it was thought that whites were superior because of the color of their skin? Have we gone back to a time of the Willie Lynch idea that the house slave was regarded as better because he or she was lighter in skin color than the darker skinned field hands? This divided black people then, and it does now as well; so much so that instead of togetherness, light skinned people and dark skinned people sometimes see each other as a threat. They are pitted against each other, and that is a direct product of the Willie Lynch slavery mentality produced by the raping of the black woman by the white slave master. Black people come in so many different shades, and we are all beautiful. We are so divided by the unimportant skin color mentality.

My experience was just a little different from that of the dark skinned woman. Our varying features can cause problems and friction amongst blacks. Being a victim of racism can exist within the same race of people, and the worst scenario can occur within our own families. I am a light skinned woman, and I come from a family of many shades. What bothered me growing up was being made fun of or being made to feel bad because of the color of my skin. One classmate nicknamed me "Dirty Red." There was nothing appealing about that, and when I confronted him about it, he said that I had a dirty red color. In another instance, a close relative loathed the color of my skin. He said, "You have the color of shit." I remember lying awake at night, wishing I could have been born with darker skin, while some black girls were wishing for lighter skin.

There are other stories of black women feeling ugly because of family members telling them their skin color was ugly. My friend, Janice, tells of how her grandmother favored her lighter skinned grandchildren over her darker skinned grandchildren. I have heard this on numerous occasions. Back in the day, some blacks would not marry a dark skinned person for fear of having black babies. Some black men today talk about their desire for lighter skinned women. Some women even bleach their skin so as not to appear dark. Some even want to deny their blackness. During the time in which I grew up, people were obsessed with skin color. In a very racist society in the southern section of these United States, there was this saying:

> If you are white, you're all right.
> If you're yellow, you're mellow.
> If you're brown, stick around.
> If you're black, get back.

This is sad. Many black girls and women had an inferiority complex about skin color, and some have continued this antiquated conceptualization of skin color. Some continue to suffer an inferiority complex. Frankly, I did not know how much concern existed about black features until I began to talk to young women and feelings were expressed. Maybe what we are exposed to in the media is causing black women to be at odds with one another. In a sense, it may also be causing divisiveness between black men and women. Light skinned women are bashing dark skinned women, and dark skinned women are bashing lighter skinned women. God does not want this conflict among black sisters.

People can be cruel, petty, and idiotic, but let us move beyond such thinking. This is told to you so that you may know that there is a division among blacks, and there need not be. Today we do not have to give ear to that attitude from people. Black women are beautiful women, and the different shades make us unique and beautiful people. Life is just too short; there is simply no time to be concerned about something as petty as skin color. Love yourself and appreciate the beauty God gave you and your sisters.

Black women sometimes are self-conscious about their curly hair. Will it allow them to progress in the professional world? So many of our celebrity black sisters are changing their hairstyles to portray what is seen in the white world as the standard for beauty, as portrayed by world media. Do not allow white America to set the standard for how you show your beauty. Do not be afraid to be beautiful as you are. My little friend, Angela, wanted to get a new hair style so that she could look like her favorite black female singer. What she must realize is that the singer's hair style and looks are not real. Now I tell you ladies: let us always rejoice in authentic beauty. We do not have to be dissatisfied with our bodies, hair, or skin color. Your beauty has nothing to do with what the world thinks. Love yourself, and know that you are beautiful. If you do not love yourself, no one else will. We do not have to reshape ourselves in anguish to conform to what society perceives as beauty. We are beautiful women. We cannot help that we live in a society that continues to have the old "Willie Lynch" mindset. The struggles of the past, which we are allowing to destroy our togetherness, have to be discontinued.

Black women do not like hearing from some ill-informed people that some black women, who are high achievers and successful, suffer from de-feminization that says they are not attractive at all. It is pathetic how women that are working hard toward self-improvement, women who have established intelligent goals and a great sense of work ethic, have been labeled unattractive "nappy-headed ho's." It was plastered all over television about how Don Imus referred to the Rutgers basketball players. There have been all kinds of talk about successful black women in the media; some sources talk about them having poor attitudes. They have been called controlling, loud, negative, aggressive, and violent. They are single mothers raising kids and are unable to be nurturing. It has been said that these women will never be loved or get married. I cannot believe that anyone can generalize about a whole segment of black women or black women in general.

There has been too much in the press about relationships between black men and black women. Some go so far as to say that a black woman is not as attractive as a white woman; therefore, black men find white women more desirable. Satoshi Kanazawa, who works in the field of evolutionary psychology, wrote an article called "Why are Black Women Less Physically Attractive Than Other Women?" This article appeared in *Psychology Today* and was later retracted. It is dangerous to make generalizations about a group of people without proof. While I am not an authority on what the black man desires, I hope it is not true that our black men are more attracted to white women. However, some matchmakers, who provide services to black men who are financially stable, report that black men prefer white blonds. There is a consensus in many circles that black men prefer white women instead of black women, especially those in the entertainment arena. Yes, some of our black men, like Bryant Gumbel, Charles Barkley, Scottie Pippen, Montel Williams, Quincy Jones, James Earl Jones, Harry Belafonte, Sydney Poitier, Kofi Anan, Cuba Gooding, Jr., Bill Blanks, Wesley Snipes, and others, are with white women. However, there are many men who are among the ranks of successful black men that desire black women. Men like Denzel Washington, Morris Chestnut, Will Smith, Blair Underwood, Samuel L. Jackson, and Chris Rock are married to strong, black women. Some white men desire black women, and they are marrying black women. Love and pray that God will send a man that you can love, and he loves you as well. I'd like to believe that there are numerous intelligent and successful black men who find black women attractive, and there is no need to look white to make them notice us.

Be confident in your attractiveness, and demand respect from men that are attracted to you. Do not sell yourself short. Expect to be treated like the beautiful woman that you are by the ones that pursue you. Be sure he is a good friend and a good person. He is to be polite, well-mannered, and able to be a good listener. Most of all, it is important to be treated well. Likewise, it is imperative that you display the same qualities. What really makes relationships work is teamwork. We are not victims of society. Bob Marley once said, "Emancipate yourselves from mental slavery. No one but ourselves can free our minds." Black women are beautiful and worthy of being loved by all. Know this to be the truth.

Do not dwell on negative information about black women in the media. Each day, life presents opportunities and new possibilities. The media is a source of income to those who indulge in these negative and undesirable comments. As long as they are making money from what they present, they will continue. The media does not know black women, and they have no idea of the tremendous strength given to them by God to endure. Black women have had a different struggle in the home, workplace, and society as a whole. We have been strong enough to survive and overcome a myriad of atrocities. What you see when looking at a successful black woman is strength, not de-feminization. Michelle Obama, like some other black, successful women, has been labeled as an angry black woman. It is not anger that she displays; it is intelligence and the ability to express an opinion that may not be in touch with what certain people embrace. Do not succumb to the rubbish in the media; they will not smother the beauty, intelligence, and possibilities you have as a magnificent black woman.

Let's review all about the beautiful you:

1. **Know that you are beautiful**
    Are you really attractive enough? Are you a beautiful woman? Yes, you are a beautiful black woman! God has created each individual in his own image. Each person is a wonderful and unique creature with talents and attributes. Even if God has never been read about, he can be seen in the blessed miracles that surround this universe. The black woman is one of those blessed miracles, and that makes you beautiful.
2. **Affirm your beauty**
    Look in the mirror each morning and say, "I am beautiful. I am a wonderfully created person. I am being a better person each day, and I truly feel good about myself." Always dress for the occasion. Surround yourself with people who love you and help you feel better about yourself. Work hard at loving and nurturing them. Do not listen to negative comments about the beauty of the black woman. Continue to say, "I am a beautiful woman."
3. **Embrace who you are**
    Do not surrender to what the world describes as the ideal look. God creates, and his creations are beautiful.

Some women surveyed thought themselves unattractive to the opposite sex because they were too fat. They grew up feeling insecure because of their weight. However, the real test is to ask, "Would losing weight make me a healthier person, extending my life?" If the answer is yes, then this is a goal for you to set. You should feel good about yourself, have high self-esteem, and be healthy. Hopefully, a male and female relationship would be one where each could forgive each other's flaws, failings, and weaknesses. Hopefully, the couple would be able to work together on self-improvement. You are a beautiful woman and you have much to offer. Many of us think we are too fat and need to lose weight. However, it is interesting to note that Halle Berry, one of *People Magazine's* fifty most beautiful people, said, "Beauty? Let me tell you something: being thought of 'as a beautiful woman' has spared me nothing in life, no heartache, no trouble. Love has been difficult," (allgreatquote.com/halle_berry_quotes.shtml).

We place too much emphasis on external beauty, and it is transitory, for it depends on youth, the powder, paints and other beautifiers we use. Love yourself. God made you the way you are.

4. **Nurture your inner beauty**
   Are you one of those women that cannot see how beautiful you are? Beauty comes from within. The world looks at beauty as how you appear externally. We are too obsessed with fashion; we should be more concerned with health and the inner self. Of course we need to be concerned with hygiene, neatness, and grooming. These things are great, but your attitude and what you think of yourself are very important. Appearance is important to us, and we spend a lot of money on improving our appearance. We need to learn how to focus on developing inner beauty. True beauty begins within, and the Bible lets us know that.

1 Samuel 16:7 says, "But the Lord said unto Samuel, 'Look not on his countenance, or on the height of his stature; because I have refused him: for the Lord seeth not as man seeth; for man looketh on the outward appearance, but the Lord looketh on the heart,'" (KJV). Samuel was charged with selecting a man for the king of Israel, but he

was looking for a man who was tall and handsome like Saul. The lesson here is that the outward appearance may not be the real person. God looks at the heart, and that is where you see the real worth of a person. The qualities possessed on the inside are very important. They include fine qualities like intelligence, compassion, kindness, grace, compassion, and a host of others. The qualities that make people beautiful are the things that people adore. Those qualities create a delightful person with a great spirit. That is called inner beauty.

Years ago, I met a woman by the name of Evelyn. Her husband's friends thought she was unattractive. They wondered why he married her, but when Evelyn came in and opened her mouth, she could light up a room. She became the most beautiful person you had ever seen. She was beautiful because of her attitude, her impeccable spirit, and her charm. That inner beauty was present, and she just glowed. Her husband's friends then realized what their friend found beautiful about his wife. I know they learned a lesson about beauty because they never called Evelyn unattractive again.

The world's view is so superficial, and we may not have all of the right things that make us physically attractive by the world's standards. Those whom we think have external beauty sometimes lack the qualities which lie on the inside that make people truly beautiful. Therefore, we should celebrate that inner beauty, for it is the true key in determining beauty. A beautiful person is made by God, and if the heart is right, you will glow as Evelyn did when I first saw her. When women similar to Evelyn display such qualities in your presence, compliment them. Take note of how her inner beauty made her a stand out. Remember beauty is shown in your actions. See how inner beauty exudes confidence, poise, charm, which is indeed attractive.

5. **Be thankful**
   Being thankful makes you beautiful inside, for it is the realization that you are a steward of God. You are then aware that all resources and all that you have come from God.

1 Chronicles 29:11–12 says,

"Thine, O Lord, is the greatness, and the power, and the glory, and the victory, and the majesty: for all that is in the heaven and in the earth is thine; thine is the kingdom, O lord, and thou art exalted as head above all. Both riches and honour come of thee, and thou reignest over all; and in thine hand is power and might; and in thine hand it is to make great, and to give strength unto all," (KJV).

David knew all he had was on loan to him from God. Whether we may enjoy money, love, security, or knowledge, it is on loan to us from God. We should thank God continually; David knew this. As black people, we have been blessed. We have moved from the throngs of slavery to freedom with opportunities now that were not available to blacks in the past. Like David, we must acknowledge God's greatness.

You must possess some other qualities that make a person beautiful:

- **Humility**
  A truly humble person is a beautiful person that is in a meaningful relationship with God and humanity. It is not important to gain recognition from people. Do not brag or boast. Treat all people well, and never feel that one person deserves more of your time and attention because of his or her importance. The Bible says in 1 Peter 5:6, "Humble yourselves therefore under the mighty hand of God, that he may exalt you in due time," (KJV). You do not have to be exalted by man. That is what God will do for you. His recognition counts more than human applause.

  Let God guide you as you walk through this life. When you are doing well, you begin to think you are great; sometimes testing and trying times come. That will teach you humility. That is the time you recognize we are "earthen vessels," (2 Corinthians 4:7, KJV). From the earth we came, and to the earth we shall return. Remain humble. Instead of showing

43

pride and self-exaltation, display humility, forget about self, and elevate the glory of God.

- **Patience**

  Patience means to suffer or endure. Hebrews 12:1 says, "Wherefore seeing we also are compassed about with so great a cloud of witnesses, let us lay aside every weight, and the sin which doth so easily beset us, and let us run with patience the race that is set before us," (KJV). Don't let the idea of patience confuse you.

  Do not sit and wait for things to happen. People have faced the same problems you face while working toward your goal. They have run the race with great strength and won. God helps you to keep going. The trials you face are placed there to perfect your patience.

  Because I am a teacher, I can talk about developing patience. Teachers develop this quality because the young adults that they deal with on a daily basis are good at trying the patience of adults. There has to be some love for them to be there for them. Thank God for the teachers. Patience is developed after going through difficult times, after which comes the calm. We learn to be patient. Patience is one of those attributes that makes you truly beautiful because it can have a tranquil effect on another and resolve difficult situations.

- **Kindness**

  Kindness can be shared by words and deeds. We have been placed in this world with other human beings, and life is so much better when we are kind and gracious to one another. Smile at someone today and allow the kindness to flow from you. Show compassion to others, and forgive them when they offend you, and then you can understand God's mercy toward us. Ephesians 4:32 says, "And be ye kind one to another, tenderhearted, forgiving one another, even as God for Christ's sake hath forgiven you," (KJV). Life is too short to be cruel or unforgiving to others. As you grow older, you will realize how short life is when friends and loved ones begin to leave this earth. Take the time now to be kind to others.

- **Joy**

  Be joyful and calm, even in difficult times. Joy is a delightful feeling developed when you feel good about yourself, when you love yourself, when you take care of yourself, and can move to the other side of your pain, because God helps you walk through harmful situations.

  Joy and happiness is not based on what is perceived as the good life. The possession of things or being able to perform well in a particular undertaking does not bring joy. Joy comes with an unceasing relationship with God. God lets you know you are not alone. John 15:11 says, "These things have I spoken unto you, that my joy might remain in you, and that your joy might be full," (KJV).

- **Remember to savor the springtime**

  I share this with you because this is something that is dear to me. Walk and enjoy the springtime and the beauty it brings. Walk and look at the beautiful flowers in spring and see the beauty in yourself. I grew up in southern Texas where the state flower is the bluebonnet. There is nothing like walking in the countryside and enjoying the color purple and all of the pinks, reds, and yellows blooming there. Have some quiet time by the water amongst the green grass, smelling the flowers, and watching the waves as they move gently in the wind while the sun sets on the horizon. Find some time and a place to relax. It's a beautiful life, you know. You are a beautiful and wonderful one. Savor the springtime by enjoying the beauty it gives externally and inwardly.

  Enjoy the beauty of this poem:

  "Beauty"
  Beauty isn't the shape of your body.
  Beauty isn't the color of your perfect eyes.
  Beauty isn't the perfectness of your face.
  Beauty is the talents that you have.
  Beauty is the intelligence that you possess.

Beauty is the way you understand me.
Your beauty is the thing that makes me smile.
Your beauty is the thing that makes me want you.
Your beauty is the thing that makes me say I love you.

Poet Unknown

We get up

In spite of all the obstacles and labels which society places upon black women, we get up. Historically, beautiful black women have done great things, and you will continue to do great things in spite of the adversities you face. Read, if you have not, some of Maya Angelou's books, which offer so much inspiration and insight to black women. Her beautiful poetry can only come from a magnificent and beautiful woman. From the throne of black women comes the first lady of the United States, Michelle Obama, who was a successful attorney in her own right before becoming the first lady. She is also a mother who believes in building independence and integrity in her daughters. She also holds her mother, who lives in the White House with the Obamas, in high regard. We black women have so much that makes us magnificent; you have so much that makes you magnificent! See yourself as a positive, self-confident, and beautiful woman, and the world will too.

Chapter 4

Conclusion

Hopefully this has been an encouragement for you to be a positive-thinking, self-confident, and beautiful black woman. Know that it is possible to possess all of the dimensions of a magnificent black woman and truly to be able to live life to the fullest satisfaction. It is God's intention that you enjoy this life that He has given.

Remember you are the product of what you think. We want to feel like the strong, empowered, and confident black women we know of, have read about, and have heard about. It is so important that you are beautiful on the inside and out. I hope I have encouraged you and emphasized enough how wonderful it is for black women to acquire the spiritual, mental, and emotional qualities that are necessary for success in life, economically or otherwise. I hope that you have gained something from this book that will encourage you to dream and to act on those dreams. Trust in God that you have the confidence and the will to pursue your goals, If you fail, you will get up and try again, for you are not afraid to fail. God gives you the strength to endure. It's about taking a chance and trusting God to succeed, for he has promised to be with you always. Surround yourself with beautiful people who have good attitudes and values, who support you, and who share your values.

Remember that God has created only beautiful people, and that includes you. Strive to be intelligent, and possess those really important things that sanction your inner beauty, which will help you progress further in life than your outward beauty. Embrace your inner beauty, which is so vital, and think less about the beauty the media displays. The black women mentioned here have led the way for the next generations. They have changed, I will say, some of the societal injustices against black women. It is still a work in process, but things are better for us because of them.

To my dear black sisters, if the positive thoughts are not present and the negative thoughts continue to occupy your mind, the job is not done. I suggest that you read this book over and over again until its thoughts and God's principles are ingrained. If the positive has replaced the negative, I celebrate with you, for you are truly on your way to great and wonderful things. Your attitude has changed, and you are ascending to new levels. You shall climb to new heights every day. God is truly proud. He loves you too much to allow you to be stagnant, and there is no limit to what you can do if you just let him guide you through this life. Always take some time out to meditate and pray. You truly are God's magnificent woman.

Be committed to living a fulfilled life with happiness. You read this book because of your desire to change, and you want to take the necessary steps to improve the way you live. Tell yourself you are a changed woman who can now soar to heights that you never knew were possible. You can now realize you do have a creative mind, and you can build the kind of future that you dream of. Black woman, most definitely, you are a dreamer; take the time to dream. Black woman, you are beautiful, unique, and inspirational. I would like to think that you are like me—ageless. The comments in this book are for black women of all ages who feel the need to improve upon their life circumstances. Just know that you have the necessary qualities to maximize your confidence and self-esteem, and your finesse is visible in spite of the often derogatory statements that we are attacked by. Black women do not have to listen to the negative statements in the media that some ill-informed people are spouting about black women. We must continue to soar in spite of innuendoes. We must know who we are, and we should continue to be strong as we exhibit our talents, our ability to survive, and as we utilize efforts to thrive and excel.

Mae C. Jemison, the first black, female astronaut who flew into space on the Endeavour space shuttle for eight days on September 12, 1992, went on to achieve additional acclaim after she left the NASA program. But she also experienced racial indignity. After being stopped for speeding by a state trooper, the trooper grasped and twisted her arm as she was thrust to the ground and handcuffed. Afterwards, she told *Newsweek* magazine, "One of the things I'm very concerned about is that as African-Americans, as women, many times we do not feel that we have the power to change the world and society as a whole." She became a medical doctor, amongst other accomplishments, and is now retired; however, she remains a tireless supporter of getting young African-American women involved in the field of science and technology.

Now embrace yourself, your beauty, your confidence, your positive thoughts, and your desire to make yourself a better woman in all areas of your life, and perhaps do something to change the world and society as a whole. You will become empowered by your efforts to excel. Love yourself and live your life like you are the greatest. You are hot! Then affirm yourself and say, "I have the confidence, I am a positive thinker, I am capable, and I am a beautiful child of God. I will walk with my head held high, for I know there is worth in me, and I step like a woman that is going somewhere, for with God I am going somewhere, and I am a successful black woman. I am a wonderful one." Affirm that you know it is important to love God, yourself, and others. Remain a spiritual being. Support, uphold, and encourage other black women to reach for excellence.

You are that flower in the Master's bouquet!

Bibliography

Allen, James. As You Think: Second Edition. The edited version by Marc Allen. Novato,CA:New World Library, 1998.

Carter, Jimmy. Sources of Strength: Meditations on Scripture for a Living Faith. U.S.A.: Times Books, 1999.

Printed in the United States
By Bookmasters